Lydia, Fashioned with Purpose

A.D. Long

Published by Interfaith University in partnership with AMC

ISBN:

CONTENTS

ACKNOWLEDGMENTS

Thank you to those who encouraged me on the journey of writing this book. You never doubted that I could do it. Thank you for never failing to show your love and support.

1 LYDIA OF THYATIRA

Lydia was a woman God fashioned with a purpose. Like many today, Lydia was in search of her identity and purpose. Although she had what many would exclaim "the perfect life," Lydia was still left unfulfilled. But her quest leads her to Christ which is the answer. Let us reflect on her journey to understanding why she was created by God and how she found hope. In order to understand Lydia's journey, we must start by looking at her background.

Lydia was the first noted and recorded European Christian convert of Apostle Paul. She is known for being a well-respected businesswoman in Philippi who was of Asiatic decent. In Hebrew, her name means "strife," and means "to travail", in the Greek. The name Lydia also means "one from the providence of Lydia" or "the Lydian woman." So, Lydia was probably not the name given to her at birth. It is popular in the Asian culture to have a name that reflects where you are from; in this regard, the name "Lydia" would be more like what we would call a nickname today. William Ramsay believes that the Lydian woman's name from birth may have been either Euodia or Syntyche.

These two Philippian women, Euodia and Syntche, were first mentioned in Philippians 4:2-3:

"[2] I beseech Euodias, and beseech Syntyche, that they be of the same mind in the Lord. [3] And I intreat thee also, true yokefellow, help those women which laboured with me in the gospel, with Clement also, and with other my fellowlabourers, whose names are in the book of life."

The name *Euodia* meant "fragrant," while *Syntche* meant "fortunate." Although little is known of their genealogy and family life, we know from Scripture that they were among the women that Paul preached the gospel to while on the riverside. He also referred to them as "co-laborers" in the gospel. Euodia and Syntche were also prosperous women who, no doubt, ministered to Paul with their substance. The Bible is unclear as to whether these two women served as official deaconesses in the church or whether their homes were just two of the houses where the church would meet. It is also recorded in scripture that these two women once had a difference of opinion. Though the topic of their quarrel is unknown, Paul encouraged both Euodia and Syntche to "be of the same mind." Their lack of unity seemed to trouble the Apostle Paul so much that he encouraged and advised them to reconcile.

By looking at the Scripture, we know that Lydia had a household. Many have concluded it was likely that Lydia was a widow. This conclusion is based on the premise that the scriptures do not indicate that Lydia consulted with her husband before inviting Apostle Paul to stay at her home. It was common in those days for women to consult with their husbands before inviting guests to stay in their homes. However, we know for sure that she had a household that included children, other relatives, and servants.

History of The Lydian People

In Genesis chapter 9, after the flood of Noah, the ark landed in the area of Mt. Ararat, which is in present-day Turkey. In that area, God commanded Noah and his sons to "be fruitful and multiply, and replenish the earth..."

The first patriarch of the Lydian dynasty is Noah. He was the first to govern this area, which was later given the name Lydia. Lud, the fourth son of Shem, was the ancestor of the now recognized Lydian people. Genesis 10:22 – "The children of Shem; Elam, and Asshur, and Arphaxad, and Lud, and Aram." Lud's descendants were the first people group to occupy the land we now know as Turkey.

The Hittites then migrated to this area and took over the land in 1900 B.C. They were direct descendants of Heth. Heth was the son of Canaan, the grandson of Ham, and the great-grandson of Noah. Genesis 10:15 – "And Canaan begot Sidon his first born, and Heth..." The earliest recorded inhibitors of the providence Turkey were the Hittite people.

They took control of the land when they conquered the local people (Lud's descendants) and established good relationships with them. After the Hittites seized Babylon in 1595 B.C., the land was taken from them in 717 B.C. by the Assyrians. When the Assyrians acquired the land, they began to call it Lu(d)du.

According to Herodotus (1.7), before receiving the name Lydia, (which is derived from Lydus, the son of Atys), the land was called Maeonia (Illad, ii, 865). The Maeonians were probably conquered by the Lydians, a tribe that resorted to the north of them. Lud is listed with Tubal and Javan, which was located around the Aegean and the Caspian Sea. This helps to settle the location of Lydia and the Lydian people.

In the 600s, Lydia was an independent country and a very prosperous kingdom. Because the country lay west of Mesopotamia and East of the Aegean Sea, it was a perfect place for commerce. The Lydians were wealth driven people. Their focus was constantly on ways to earn and circulate money within their providence. Lydians were the first group of people to create their own coin, which was called *staters* (meaning standard). This Lydian currency was made of a gold and silver mixture called electrum.

Lud vs. Ludium

There has been great confusion as to whether the Lydians are descendants of Lud, Shem's son, or Ludium, Ham's grandson. I discovered that there was a Semitic Lud and a Hematic Lud and that there were Lydians in Africa and Asia Minor. From my research, I have concluded two explanations for this encounter. We could reason that because Africa (Ludium) and Asia Minor (Lud) are in two different localities, they are two separate nations with similar names. And secondly, we could see Lydians in Africa and Asia Minor as a result of the Egyptians hiring the Lydians as mercenaries in 663-609 B.C by King Gyges. They were hired to fight against the Assyrians in Psameticus. It is possible that some of the

Lydians migrated to Africa and moved their families to this area.

Thyatira, Lydia's Hometown

The providence of Lydia contained the cities of Ephesus, Smyrna, Pergamum, Thyatira, Sardis, Philadelphia, and Laodicea. Lydia was originally from the Lydian providence Thyatira. It was located on the outskirts of Lydia and Mysia. Today, Thyatira is known as Ak-Hissar, which means "white castle." This providence was well known as a prodigious trade city and was world-renowned for dyeing textiles. Inscriptions can be found among the ruins of ancient Thyatira from the dyer's guild. It was a very affluent and flourishing region. Like the other cities in

Lydia, Thyatira was a "melting pot of different nations."

2 LYDIA'S PROFESSION

Lydia was known for being a "seller of purple," Acts 16:14 – "And a certain woman named Lydia, a seller of purple, of the city of Thyatira, which worshipped God, heard us..." Her profession would be equivalent to the fashion industry today. Before it became popular to cut and shape clothing in the way that we do today, those who supplied the material to wrap or make clothing were high in demand. Lydia sold this renown dye and/or dyed cloth that was used for both clothing and decorating. There were several names for this dye: *Tyrian purple, Tyrian red, royal purple, imperial purple* or *imperial dye*. The dye was greatly valued in these times because it did not quickly weather and fade like other dyes. As a result, the color would remain vibrant for a long time. This Tyrian purple was a dye used when coloring fabrics for the tabernacle. The other dye Thyatira produced, which was blue, was also retrieved from a *tekhelet*, a sea snail. This dye was also costly and regal.

The Occupation of Dying

Dying has been among the top occupations since the Old Testament. Although the dying process is not described in the Old Testament, the Israelites have been familiar with dying items since the earliest times in history. Purple, crimson, and blue dyes were most often used on cloth. Purple dye was worn symbolically as a staple of wealth and royalty. Texts and remains have been found of a dyeing business that dates to early 1500 B.C. This establishment seems to have been utilized by the Canaanites and located in Ugarit, Syria.

There were various ways that the notorious purple, crimson, and blue dyes were created.

1.   The Phoenicians reserved the secret of how they created their blue and purple pigments from shellfish. It was later discovered that the dye was obtained from the gland of the mollusk. Depending on the

exposure of light and any added ingredients, the dye would become lighter or darker (Ezekiel 27:7, 16, 24).

Ezekiel 27:7 – "Fine linen with broidered work from Egypt was that which thou spreadest forth to be sail; blue and purple from the isles of Elishah was that which covered thee."

Ezekiel 27:16 – "Syria was thy merchant by reason of the multitude of the wares of the making: they occupied in thy fairs with emeralds, purple, and broidered work, ad fine linen, and coral, and agate."

Ezekiel 27:24 – "These were thy merchants in all sorts of things, in blue clothes, and broidered work, and in chests of rich apparel, bound with cords, and made of cedar, among merchandise."

2.   Crimson and scarlet dyes were taken from the *kermes* or *cohineal* insect. This insect feeds on oak located in Turkey and Southern Europe. Rams' skin covered in crimson dye was used in the building of the tabernacle. This same dye is still being utilized to cover leather made objects today.

3.   The Lydians used a "madder root," instead of the mollusk fish, to create the exquisite Tyrian purple. The water in Thyatira was well acclimatized for dyeing. As a result of the water, no other people group could yield the imperial purple like the Lydians. The water allotted the cloth to be permanently dyed with

an elaborate and unique color. In this case, Lydia was universally renowned for producing this lovely imperial dye. Today, this region still produces Tyrian purple. However, the dye today is created from the excretion of a *predacious Murex*.

Trade Guilds

In Lydia, trade guilds were vital to being in business, especially for those in Thyatira. Lydia's hometown was noted for its trade guilds, which were more organized than any other guilds located in other cities.

Trade guilds were incorporated organizations that were categorized as either a merchant or craft guild. Merchant guilds were unions of merchants in a particular area, town, or city.

Whether a local or long-distance trader (usually men), were sellers and traders of an assortment of goods. Craft guilds were completely different from merchant guilds. Craft guilds served as work-related unions or associations that generally consisted of all the "artisans and craftsmen" in a more specific division of industry or business, i.e. "guilds of dyers and weavers in the wool trade, masons and architects in building trade."

During this time, guilds presented a diversity of significant purposes in the local economy. They formed the domination of trade locally or within a specific division of industry or business. Criteria were set and maintained to ensure the quality of goods and the reliability of trading practices in that area of business.

Guilds also worked to ensure unchanging prices for their merchandising. They also pursued ways to get control of "town or city governments" to advance the guild members' welfare and accomplish their economic intents.

All artisans had to be affiliated with a guild. Each guild had its property, was revered and respected, and completed major jobs. Everyone associated with a trade guild had a great deal of influence. The most popular guilds were the coppersmiths and the dyers guild. Lydia was affiliated with the dyer's guild. Although the Bible is not clear as to whether she sold purple dye or purple-dyed cloth, Lydia was the "seller of purple" and served as a representative for the trade guild in Philippi. It was the job of each trade representative to seek recruits for their guild. These associations were very appealing to join because they promised that one would be well-known and respected in the business. Anyone successful in business during that time attributed their wealth to that alliance.

When entering the association, one had to submit to the god(s) and rituals of that organization. Refusal to do so meant that the individual could no longer be apart. It is essential to note that those, like Lydia, who accepted Christ and became Christians, had to renounce their associations with their guilds to receive Christ wholeheartedly. "It was taught by many of the early church that no Christian might belong to one of the guilds, and thus the greatest opposition to Christianity was presented." This alliance proved to be a great problem in the church in Thyatira. Many tried to hold fast to their alliance with their guild and serve God. Some Thyatirans found this very hard because they had to be affiliated with one of these organizations to make their living.

If one wanted to disassociate with their guild, one had to give up the connections gained from being in the guild. One can imagine the risk Lydia took by relinquishing her ties with the dyers and accepting Christ wholeheartedly. She was saying to God that He mattered more than her earthly success, wealth, and business. By doing so, Lydia was still considered prosperous and served God with her whole heart. Some Thyatirian Christians struggled to give up their alliances, and it greatly affected their walk with God. However, Lydia is a great example that no matter what alliance one had before Christ, if trust is placed in Him, prosperity will come because of obedience to his word.

3 PAUL, THE MESSENGER

Paul was the man God chose to bring Lydia into the knowledge of Him. Through Paul, Lydia learned about God and His divine kingdom.

Paul's background and conversion prepared him to minister to others. Originally named Saul, Paul was an authentic Jew of the tribe of Benjamin. He was learned in the Aramaic language and a devout Pharisee by tradition. As a Pharisee, Paul was a meticulous observer of the requisites of the Torah. Because he was of Jewess decent, he had advanced in Judaism beyond all of his colleagues. He was born in Tarsus of Cilicia, which was the center of Greek culture. It was also known as "a place of education and commerce." According to Ramsey, Tarsus was "the city whose institutions best and most completely united the oriental and the western character." In his late teens, Paul then moved to Jerusalem. There he was educated by Gamaliel.

Paul's Conversion

Paul's conversion is recorded in Acts, chapter 9. Acts 9:1-19:

¹ "And Saul, yet breathing out threatenings and slaughter against the disciples of the Lord, went unto the high priest,

² And desired of him letters to Damascus to the synagogues, that if he found any of this way, whether they were men or women, he might bring them bound unto Jerusalem.

³ And as he journeyed, he came near Damascus: and suddenly there shined round about him a light from heaven:

⁴ And he fell to the earth, and heard a voice saying unto him, Saul, Saul, why persecutest thou me?

⁵ And he said, Who art thou, Lord? And the Lord said, I am Jesus whom thou persecutest: it is hard for thee to kick against the pricks.

⁶ And he trembling and astonished said, Lord, what wilt thou have me to do? And the Lord said unto him, Arise, and go into the city, and it shall be told thee what thou must do.

⁷ And the men which journeyed with him stood speechless, hearing a voice, but seeing no man.

⁸ And Saul arose from the earth; and when his eyes were opened, he saw no man: but they led him by the hand, and brought him into Damascus.

⁹ And he was three days without sight, and neither did eat nor drink.

¹⁰ And there was a certain disciple at Damascus, named Ananias; and to him said

the Lord in a vision, Ananias. And he said, Behold, I am here, Lord.

11 And the Lord said unto him, Arise, and go into the street which is called Straight, and enquire in the house of Judas for one called Saul, of Tarsus: for, behold, he prayeth,

12 And hath seen in a vision a man named Ananias coming in, and putting his hand on him, that he might receive his sight.

13 Then Ananias answered, Lord, I have heard by many of this man, how much evil he hath done to thy saints at Jerusalem:

14 And here he hath authority from the chief priests to bind all that call on thy name.

15 But the Lord said unto him, Go thy way: for he is a chosen vessel unto me, to bear my

name before the Gentiles, and kings, and the children of Israel:

¹⁶ For I will shew him how great things he must suffer for my name's sake.

¹⁷ And Ananias went his way, and entered into the house; and putting his hands on him said, Brother Saul, the Lord, even Jesus, that appeared unto thee in the way as thou camest, hath sent me, that thou mightest receive thy sight, and be filled with the Holy Ghost.

¹⁸ And immediately there fell from his eyes as it had been scales: and he received sight forthwith, and arose, and was baptized.

[19] And when he had received meat, he was strengthened. Then was Saul certain days with the disciples which were at Damascus."

Saul went to the high priest and requested letters to take to Damascus to persecute Christians in the area and brought them to Jerusalem for judgment. As he went on his journey, a light shined bright around him from heaven. After seeing this bright blinding light, he fell off his horse, and he heard the voice of Jesus. Jesus called his name and asked Paul why he persecuted Him. Paul, astonished, and trembling, asked: "Lord, what wilt thou have me do?" The Lord then instructed him to go into the city, and he will get further instructions. Although he was blinded by the bright light, Paul arose as instructed and went into the city. When he reached Damascus, he met Ananias (whom God had already spoken to about Paul). God told Ananias that he had chosen Paul to "bear his name before the Gentiles, and the kings, and the children of Israel." In Damascus, Paul's sight was recovered; he was baptized and was filled with the Holy Ghost. He then began to preach the gospel in the synagogue in Damascus. (In his letter to the Galatians, Paul also discussed his conversion.)

Paul's Missionary Journeys

Paul's missionary journeys covered a span of about ten years. His work was predominantly in Galatia, Macedonia, Achaia, and Asia (primarily Roman providences). Paul always focused on the main cities of each providence he visited and then branched out to surrounding countries. He often reached those in surrounding countries by utilizing the locals who were converted to Christianity (i.e., Epaphras, etc.).

Paul's method of starting churches can be seen in Acts 14.

Acts 14:21-23 – "21 And when they had preached the gospel to that city, and had taught many, they returned again to Lystra, and to Iconium, and Antioch,

22 Confirming the souls of the disciples, and exhorting them to continue in the faith, and that we must through much tribulation enter into the kingdom of God.

[23] And when they had ordained them elders in every church, and had prayed with fasting, they commended them to the Lord, on whom they believed."

Paul's method was to (1) evangelize, (2) edify, (3) organize. He always went into an area preaching the gospel. After making sure that those who were newly converted had a sure foundation of the word, he then began strengthening and encouraging the believers in that locality. Lastly, Paul appointed those he saw as mature in that area as elders of that local church.

His Missionary Trip to Macedonia

Paul's second missionary journey was first intended to be used as a time to revisit the places where he had already ministered. Instead, the center of his focus became Macedonia and Achaia. Once passing through Lystra, Timothy and Paul came to Troas. After seeing a vision of a Macedonian man needing help, he endeavored to Macedonia.

Paul mainly focused his ministerial work in three Macedonian cities, Philippi, Thessalonica, and Berea. The Gentiles were often the first to respond to the gospel and receive salvation. In Philippi, Paul encountered those who feared God. Paul taught "the doctrine of justification by faith" and "the concept of being in Christ." The doctrine of justification by faith was at the core of Paul's messages. After having experienced it in his own life, it became introductory in his letters to the churches. This is evident in the letters written to the Galatians and Romans. The doctrine of justification through faith emphasizes that "man is given right standing with God through faith, rather than as a result of his own meritorious." Ephesians 2:8--- "For by grace are ye saved through faith; and that not of yourselves: it is the gift of God:" Paul also expressed through his teachings that being "in Christ" meant liberty from the bondage of sin and the law. Paul never neglected to speak about the expectancy of Christ's return. He looked forward to the second advent of Christ.

The Man in Paul's Vision

One of the most important parts of this Missionary journey is the vision Paul had which caused him to further reconsider his course. I repeatedly asked myself, "Why was there a man in Paul's Macedonian vision, but when he arrived in Philippi, he met Lydia, a woman?" Well, some scholars and historians believe that if we take a closer look at Acts 16, we can get some clue as to who this Macedonian man might have been. Acts 16:9-10 says, "9 And a vision appeared to Paul in the night; There stood a man of Macedonia, and prayed him, saying, Come over into Macedonia, and help us.

10 And after he had seen the vision, immediately we endeavored to go into Macedonia, assuredly gathering that the Lord had called us for to preach the gospel unto them."

William Ramsay, a historian, believed that Luke was the man in the Macedonian dream. Luke was a physician, author, and companion of Paul. He was the writer of the third Gospel and the book of Acts.

Ramsay believed Luke was the man in the Macedonian vision for several reasons:

1.   He believed that Luke met Apostle Paul just before he had this vision. Acts 16:8 says, "And they passing by Mysia came down to Troas." It is believed that at some point of reaching Troas, Apostle Paul must have met Luke because in Acts 16:10 it says that "we endevoured to go into Macedonia." This is the first time that Luke uses "we" which attempts

to include himself into the journey with Paul, Silas, and Timothy.

2. There is no cultural or distinctive difference strictly by appearance of the Macedonians from other Roman cities. Now, when we look further at the Macedonian people, there was no particular dress or anything that could be specifically attributed to make them stand out from other Romans. They wore the typical attire that most Romans wore; and there was nothing special about their appearance that would say they were Macedonian. So, the person in the dream had to be an individual Paul had seen before or knew to some degree, either someone who was from or lived in Macedonia. In this case, Luke must have lived in Philippi.

3.   When one looks at the original Greek manuscript of the book of Acts, Luke speaks of the scene of the woman on the riverside in a way more common. He describes it in a way that only an individual who lived in the area or knew of the place could explain it.

4.   Lastly, let us consider the method God often used to direct Paul on his missionary journeys. God would often send the individual and then send the Apostle to the area that person was from. By meeting Luke first, God was showing Paul who He was going to use him to reach. Luke was a Gentile, proselyte, and a physician. Paul, a businessman, met other businesspeople and was able to lead them to Christ.

In this, we can see how much each of us mean to God. As He did with Lydia, God sent people her way to explain the gospel which helped her to understand her purpose and calling. Paul's journey and the people he met along the way prepared him to be a vessel God could use to reach out to many.

4 WHAT IS PURPOSE?

Before going any further, I would like to define the words *purpose* and *calling*. These two words are commonly used incorrectly; and for us to truly understand Lydia's story and where God is taking each of us, we must get an understanding of what we are seeking God for.

Everyone in life, whether out loud or to themselves, has a longing to understand their purpose. In this we are seeking to identify ourselves, where we want to go in life and what we ought to be. I believe that the longing to understand this part of our lives is the yearning we have for our Father in heaven. If an individual follows this quest to understand their purpose properly, it will lead them straight back to Him. Before we delve into the other portions on this topic of purpose, let us dissect what this word truly means. It is very important to define this word so that we can get down to the foundation of what purpose is all about.

According to the *Cambridge Dictionary,* the word purpose is defined as "why one does something or why something exists." For example, someone may conduct research with the purpose of understanding how the human blood flows to the arteries or a person moving to a new city for the expressed purpose of being closer to a friend. It is the *reason* something exists or the reason an individual does something a particular way. The Cambridge dictionary goes on to describe the word purpose as determination or feeling of having a reason for what ones wants to do, it can also be defined as a *need*. The *Merriam Webster Dictionary* defines purpose as something set up as an object or end to be attained: intention, resolution, determination, a subject under discussion or an action in course of execution, and by intent.

I believe God put this longing in our hearts so that we can find Him in the end. I strongly believe all humans have a longing to get a full understanding of why they exist, they want to know the intention God had for creating them or why they were placed on this earth. This is what intrigued me while doing the study on Lydia. She was a very successful and wealthy woman who was described in the book of Acts and Philippians. She was a seller of purple. Her job would be equivalent to someone in our clothing industry today. To have the occupation, Lydia had to join a dyer guild and those within that guild had to submit to the gods and rituals spelled. Those who sold the beautiful purple cloth had great influence within their communities. This occupation was well respected. It is unknown whether she had a husband, but we know that she had a household. Even with all the wealth and power she possessed, Lydia was still unfulfilled. This began her search for her purpose, which started her quest to find God. Luke made a point to describe Lydia as a "worshipper of God." She was found by the riverside with other women praying.

Define Purpose

We were all fashioned by God for a purpose, one purpose. Finding your purpose is easy because it is the same as mine, your sister's, your teacher's, and every other person on earth. Before you just close the book and refuse to go any further, let me explain through scripture.

We must first settle that God has chosen us to be a part of Him. Before we ever existed on earth, God placed us all here with a purpose in mind. Jeremiah 29:11 says, "For I know the thoughts that I think toward you, saith the LORD, thoughts of peace, and not of evil, to give you an expected end." God has chosen us to be a part of Him. John 15:16 says "Ye have not chosen me, but I have chosen you, and ordained you, that ye should go and bring forth fruit, and that your fruit should remain: that whatsoever ye shall ask of the Father in my name, he may give it you."

Isaiah 43:7 says, "Even every one that is called by my name: for I have created him for my glory, I have formed him; yea, I have made him."

Romans 8:28 – "And we know that all things work together for good to them that love God, to them who are the called according to his purpose."

In the beginning, God created us all for Him. He designed/fashioned us with the ability to make choices. He did not make us robots but gave us the ability to decide our paths in life. He did what every good parent would do. God gave us His word and provided us everything we needed to make the right decisions. However, in Gen. 3, we see that man sinned. He made the wrong choice, but God's grace still abounded on mankind's' behalf. God eventually sent His only son, Jesus, to be an example of what He desired us all to be. Jesus was the only one that got pleasing our Father in heaven accurate. John 3:16–For God so loved the world, that He *gave* his *only* Son, that whoever believes in him should not perish but have eternal life. So, God sacrificed Jesus and showed us through him, what He wanted us all to become. Luke 9:35: "And there came a voice out of the cloud, saying, This is my beloved Son: hear him."

Romans 8:29– "For whom he did foreknow, he also did predestinate to be conformed to the image of his Son, that he might be the firstborn among many brethren."

This was God's purpose for man, to be just like Christ. What did Christ do?

1.   Christ's desire above everything was to do the will of his Father. No matter what came his way or what others sought to say or do to

Christ, he wanted to please God. Jesus revealed God as our Father and lead us back Him. He was to do this by ultimately being that sacrifice and dying for our sins. Christ was so willing to complete God's will that he prayed in the Garden of Gethsemane (Matthew 26:39) "And he went a little farther, and fell on his face, and prayed, saying, O my Father, if it is possible, let this cup pass from me: nevertheless, not as I will, but as thou wilt."

Some interpret this passage to mean that Christ was scared or worried because he knew his time was near. However, this interpretation is incorrect. One can see Christ's eagerness to do what God wanted him to do; he just wanted to be sure that he was not stepping outside the appointed time stepping out of timing.

2.   Christ knew God's will and always consulted his Father through prayer before making decisions. Matthew 6:9-10 – [9] After this manner therefore pray ye: Our Father who art in heaven, Hallowed be thy name. [10] Thy kingdom come. Thy will be done in earth as it is in heaven.

3.   Christ humbled himself as a servant (dedicated his life to helping others) (we will discuss this point more in Chapter 6).

These are just a few examples of some characteristics Christ exhibited while on earth. By looking more closely at his life and studying God's word, we can get a better understanding of the purpose our Father designed us all for.

Define Calling

Many use the words purpose and calling interchangeably, and this is incorrect. One's calling has everything to do with what they are specifically designed to do. A calling would better describe a person's vocation, or occupation. God can use our calling or occupation to help us accomplish His will (purpose) for our lives. Each of our callings give us more specific ways to reach others and accomplish our ultimate purpose of being like our Jesus.

Well, how do would one determine what occupation they should be in? By accessing one's *SHAPE* (spiritual gifts, heart's desire, abilities, personality, and experience), a greater understanding of the vocation can be discovered.

1.   **Spiritual Gifts**: There are 3 ways that someone can receive gifts: 1. having a knack, or a natural ability to do something, 2. acquiring or learning the gift, and/or 3. through the Holy Spirit manifesting the gifts or abilities. When we accept Christ as our Lord and receive the Holy Spirit, God can then impart spiritual gifts or abilities to us. Such abilities are not controlled by us but are made manifest as God wills through the Holy Spirit. Roman 12:4-8 – " [4] For as we have many members in one body, and all members have not the same office:

[5] So we, being many, are one body in Christ, and every one members one of another.

[6] Having then gifts differing according to the grace that is given to us, whether prophecy, let us prophesy according to the proportion of faith;

[7] Or ministry, let us wait on our ministering: or he that teacheth, on teaching;

[8] Or he that exhorteth, on exhortation: he that giveth, let him do it with simplicity; he that ruleth, with diligence; he that showeth mercy, with cheerfulness."2.   **Abilities**:   One's abilities would be something that comes naturally to them. Such abilities or gift just comes naturally to that individual whether it be a skill from an early age or a learned skill.

For example: some have a knack to dance, sing, write, lead, speak, organize, etc.

3.   **Heart's Desire**: One's heart's desire would entail what the individual has a passion for. Their heart's desire would be something that they would do even if they were not paid for it. For example, some visual artists would paint even if they never were paid, some chefs would continue to prepare meals even if they never heard a thank you or received a tip.

4.   **Personality**: One's personality would entail the characteristics and qualities that make up who they are. For example, some may exude a more serious personality, while others tend to be more humorous. We all have varying personalities, so it is important that we select the appropriate fields that match our

personality. I have encountered individuals who chose occupations that were not befitting for their personality. For ex. A teacher with no patience, a nurse with no nurturing ability, a salesperson who does not like to engage people. These scenarios do not match the personality one would hope to find. Remember, befitting personalities matters when entering a field.

5. **Experience**: One's experience is a collection of what a person has done in the past. It is based on what they have always done, and what they usually find themselves continuing to do.

Your SHAPE helps you to fulfill God's purpose. Lydia's vocation was an avenue God used to help Lydia discover her purpose. As we began to discuss Lydia's conversion, in chapter 5, we will discover Lydia's SHAPE.

5 LYDIA'S CONVERSION

Lydia was a proselyte. We know from scripture that she was a "worshiper of God" in Acts 16:14 – "And a certain woman named Lydia, a seller of purple, of the city of Thyatira, which worshipped God, heard us: whose heart the Lord opened, that she attended unto the things which were spoken of Paul." While in Philippi, we can see that Lydia was a religious woman. She went with the other Jewish women to pray on the riverside daily. It is unknown whether there were other women,

Lydia fellowshipped with women that were proselytes. During this time, many women were searching for the true God because they were tired of the polytheism and heathenism of their countries. Some women on this quest also became Jewish proselytes. According to Josephus, (to become a Jewish proselyte), one was to accept the Jewish customs, adhere to the laws of the Jewish people and worship God as the Jews did. Before meeting Paul, Lydia had already gone through this process and converted to Judaism.

Lydia Meets Paul

The Bible discusses Paul's call to Macedonia in Acts 16:9-10 – "[9] And a vision appeared to Paul in the night; There stood a man of Macedonia, and prayed him, saying, Come over into Macedonia, and help us.

[10] And after he had seen the vision, immediately we endeavored to go into Macedonia, assuredly gathering that the Lord had called us for to preach the gospel unto them."

When Paul came from Mysia and to Troas, he had a vision in the night. In the vision, Paul saw a man beckoning him to come to Macedonia and help the people there. "…come over and help us." This marks Paul's second missionary journey. The Bible says that he immediately endeavored to go into Macedonia.

Lydia Finds Her Call

Lydia, like many today, was searching for her purpose "Why am I here?" "Why do I have the job I have?" "What can I do to help others?" This space of thinking, this moment and quest is the place in our hearts for God. It is in this query that God will step in and show us that purpose, but only if we yield to Him. It was through listening to the Apostle teach that Lydia gained an understanding of her purpose. We all have that very same purpose, which is to be *conformed to the image of Christ.*

Romans 8:28-30 – "[28] And we know that all things work together for good to them that love God, to them who are the called according to his purpose.

[29] For whom he did foreknow, he also did predestinate to be conformed to the image of his Son, that he might be the firstborn among many brethren.

[30] Moreover whom he did predestinate, them he also called: and whom he called, them he also justified: and whom he justified, them he also glorified."

So, after her searching, God opened her heart to receive what was said by the man of God, then she confessed Jesus as her savior. Now, she knows her purpose and began to tell others, starting with her household, about this Christ that she just received. She also opened her home and thus the first church in Philippi was birthed.

Next, after knowing one's purpose many want to know what I should do. God fashioned us and designed us for a specific reason. Our fashion or our deign was given to us by God so that we can accomplish His purpose for us all. Lydia had a background of being a successful businesswoman, a recruiter, and hospitable (we can tell by the way she treated the Apostle and those with him). With all this going on, Lydia's spiritual call was to be an Evangelist.

Women were always seen in the Bible as one of the great recruiters for Christ. They were great at going out and telling others about an apostle or teacher that they were listening to and leading others to hear that teacher. I believe God caused Paul to meet Lydia because He wanted to use Lydia to bring others to hear Paul Remember, before coming to Christ, Lydia was known for recruiting for her guild, but she could now use the skill of getting peoples' attention and direct them to Christ. Her call was evangelist. She shared Christ with others (men and women), starting with those she knew, her household. Although they were not as fortunate to have the technology we have today, the gospel spread like a fire across the world. It all happened by word of mouth. The Wycliffe bible dictionary stated that "The gospel brought a revolution in the status of women… After Christ's resurrection, the women united with the other disciples in prayer and full fellowship."

Acts 1:14 –"These all continued with one accord in prayer and supplication, with the women, and Mary, the mother of Jesus, and with his brethren."

They received the Holy Spirit along with men on the day of Pentecost. Acts 2:1-11– "And when the day of Pentecost was fully come, they were all with one accord in one place.

2 And suddenly there came a sound from heaven as of a rushing mighty wind, and it filled all the house where they were sitting.

3 And there appeared unto them cloven tongues like as of fire, and it sat upon each of them.

⁴ And they were all filled with the Holy Ghost, and began to speak with other tongues, as the Spirit gave them utterance.

⁵ And there were dwelling at Jerusalem Jews, devout men, out of every nation under heaven.

⁶ Now when this was noised abroad, the multitude came together, and were confounded, because that every man heard them speak in his own language.

⁷ And they were all amazed and marvelled, saying one to another, Behold, are not all these which speak Galilaeans?

⁸ And how hear we every man in our own tongue, wherein we were born?

[9] Parthians, and Medes, and Elamites, and the dwellers in Mesopotamia, and in Judaea, and Cappadocia, in Pontus, and Asia,

[10] Phrygia, and Pamphylia, in Egypt, and in the parts of Libya about Cyrene, and strangers of Rome, Jews and proselytes,

[11] Cretes and Arabians, we do hear them speak in our tongues the wonderful works of God."

Acts 2:17-18 – "17 And it shall come to pass in the last days, saith God, I will pour out of my Spirit upon all flesh: and your sons and your daughters shall prophesy, and your young men shall see visions, and your old men shall dream dreams:

[18] And on my servants and on my handmaidens I will pour out in those days of my Spirit; and they shall prophesy:"

In the life of the early Churches women were always among the first believers.

Acts 5:14 – "And believers were the more added to the Lord, multitudes both of men and women.)

Acts 12:12 – "And when he had considered the thing, he came to the house of Mary the mother of John, whose surname was Mark; where many were gathered together praying.

Acts 16:14-15 – "14 And a certain woman named Lydia, a seller of purple, of the city of Thyatira, which worshipped God, heard us: whose heart the Lord opened, that she attended unto the things which were spoken of Paul.

[15] And when she was baptized, and her household, she besought us, saying, If ye have judged me to be faithful to the Lord, come into my house, and abide there. And she constrained us."

Some like Lydia, Priscilla, and Phoebe were outstanding as fellow-workers with Paul and as women in whose homes churches met.

Rom 16:1-5 – "Then came he to Derbe and Lystra: and, behold, a certain disciple was there, named Timotheus, the son of a certain woman, which was a Jewess, and believed; but his father was a Greek:

[2] Which was well reported of by the brethren that were at Lystra and Iconium.

[3] Him would Paul have to go forth with him; and took and circumcised him because of the Jews which were in those quarters: for they knew all that his father was a Greek.

[4] And as they went through the cities, they delivered them the decrees for to keep, that were ordained of the apostles and elders which were at Jerusalem.

[5] And so were the churches established in the faith, and increased in number daily."

Apparently, there was a considerable number of Jewish women in Philippi and not a lot of men seeking God. This can be concluded because there was no synagogue in the area.

According to Jewish law, a synagogue can only be formed when ten male heads of households could attend the synagogue regularly. If this was not in place, they would pray outside near a river or a sea. This is why Lydia and the other women were found praying on the riverside.

Philippi, Paul's First Macedonian City

Philippi was located in western Thrace and was approximately 8 miles away from the coast of the Aegean Sea on what we know now as the Balkan Peninsula. The city of Philippi was constructed between 358 and 357 B.C. It was originally founded by the father of Alexander the Great, Philip II of Macedon. After defeating the Persians in 168 B.C.,

Philippi became a part of the Roman Empire. Philippi was considered a "miniature Rome," where the citizens were predominately Roman. The term Roman included all who obtained Roman citizenship. Roman citizens were privileged to have certain rights: "freedom from scourging, arrest (in cases that were not extreme), and the right to appeal to the Emperor." The language primarily spoken in Philippi was Latin. The affairs of the land where regulated by Praetors, which were Roman officials or magistrates. If you were not a citizen of Rome, you would be considered a stranger. There were a limited number of Jews in Rome, so the Jews did not have a synagogue to worship in Philippi. It is believed that they had a Proseuchae. This impermanent structure must have rested by the bank of the Gaggitas River. Philippi was the first European city that Paul visited.

Lydia's Response to The Gospel

After hearing and receiving the gospel, we can see that Lydia immediately went out and communicated what she heard from Paul to those in her household. There were some steps to Lydia's conversion that I would like to emphasize.

In Thyatira, people were all about gaining wealth and status. Lydia, like those of her hometown, was focused on having a successful life. She was both successful in business and possibly had all her money could buy. Nevertheless, Lydia wanted more than just those things. She began changing her religious practices like many women during this time. Some were simply tired of the polytheism they witnessed among their people and were seeking a better way of life. She began congregating and praying with the Jewish women at the riverside.

Much of what Lydia learned from the Jewish people was strictly religious and intellectual. As a "worshiper of God," Lydia had the fear of God but lacked an understanding of Him. "In these prayer gatherings, the women would have been reciting prayers and reading from the law and the prophets, they would discuss what they had read, and hope to hear from a traveling Jewish teacher who would bring an exposition or exhortation and receive a blessing (Article "The Lydia Factor- Go And Do It")." Imagine the women sitting on the riverside anticipating a traveling Jewish teacher to bring an exciting exhortation and they meet Paul who began to speak. Now Lydia was used to just hearing the religious and intellectual part of Judaism, but when she saw and heard Paul speak, God opened her heart to the word so that she could comprehend it and respond. She was used to hearing the Jews simply talk about a savior that was to come back and deliver the Jewish people. But when Lydia heard Paul speak about Jesus and realized that He was the savior they were anticipating, the promised messiah, she then decided to give her heart to Christ.

After her heart was opened to hear what Paul was saying, Lydia was quick to respond to the gospel. Lydia first converted to Christianity by confessing Jesus as her Lord and personal savior. Secondly, she was baptized, which is very important after there is a conversion. Baptism symbolizes the burial of the old man and the coming into a new life with Christ. She then put her attention on serving the people of God. She opened her home to the Apostle Paul and told all in her household about Christ. By opening her home to the Apostle and the church in Philippi, others were able to hear the gospel in that area. Her home was the first church established by Apostle Paul in the Macedonian providence. Lydia's home was no doubt where the letters for the Philippians were sent. It was a great center of worship and outreach in Philippi. This church had a special place in Paul's heart. The Philippians not only encouraged Paul, but they also ministered to his needs. The church grew massively because of these factors.

6 LYDIA, A TYPE OF CHRIST

Lydia had the heart to serve, just like Christ. No matter the cost, they both wanted to please God. Lydia did not consider the shame that would come by associating with Paul and the other Christians. Even as Christ despised the shame for us all. Despite it all, Lydia still served and helped the Apostle in his endeavors. After Paul and Silas were imprisoned, Lydia, along with the other Christian women in Philippi, no doubt even went to see Paul in prison. This would be considered a shameful act for a woman of Lydia's caliber. The notion of being seen with a prisoner, yet along with two, would have brought great shame to a person who held great status in the community. Even her identification with the Apostle and the disciples would have been considered ostracism. However, she was not concern about her social standing. Instead, Lydia's concern was for God's ministers, and she made sure they had the proper care they needed. Service was the most important thing for Lydia.

Christ forgot about the shame and came to save us all. He was the second person of the Godhead made flesh. Jesus, the Son of God, submitted himself as a servant and gave himself so that we could have eternal life.

Christ, the creator of all things, become a servant and associated with those who would be considered lower than him.

Philippians 2:5-8 – "5 Let this mind be in you, which was also in Christ Jesus:

6 Who, being in the form of God, thought it not robbery to be equal with God:

7 But made himself of no reputation, and took upon him the form of a servant, and was made in the likeness of men:

8 And being found in fashion as a man, he humbled himself, and became obedient unto death, even the death of the cross.

John 13:12-17 –12 So after he had washed their feet, and had taken his garments, and was set down again, he said unto them, Know ye what I have done to you?

13 Ye call me Master and Lord: and ye say well; for so I am.

14 If I then, your Lord and Master, have washed your feet; ye also ought to wash one another's feet.

15 For I have given you an example, that ye should do as I have done to you.

16 Verily, verily, I say unto you, The servant is not greater than his Lord; neither he that is sent greater than he that sent him.

17 If ye know these things, happy are ye if ye do them.

John 13:4-8 –4 He riseth from supper, and laid aside his garments; and took a towel, and girded himself.

5 After that he poureth water into a bason, and began to wash the disciples' feet, and to wipe them with the towel wherewith he was girded.

6 Then cometh he to Simon Peter: and Peter saith unto him, Lord, dost thou wash my feet?

7 Jesus answered and said unto him, What I do thou knowest not now; but thou shalt know hereafter.

8 Peter saith unto him, Thou shalt never wash my feet. Jesus answered him, If I wash thee not, thou hast no part with me."

Mark 10:45 – "For even the Son of man came not to be ministered unto, but to minister, and to give his life a ransom for many."

Luke 22:24-27---"24 And there was also a strife among them, which of them should be accounted the greatest.

25 And he said unto them, The kings of the Gentiles exercise lordship over them; and they that exercise authority upon them are called benefactors.

26 But ye shall not be so: but he that is greatest among you, let him be as the younger; and he that is chief, as he that doth serve.

27 For whether is greater, he that sitteth at meat, or he that serveth? is not he that sitteth

at meat? but I am among you as he that serveth."

Hebrews 2:17 – "Wherefore in all things it behoved him to be made like unto his brethren, that he might be a merciful and faithful high priest in things about God, to make reconciliation for the sins of the people." Jesus was never concerned about how he appeared in the eyes of his peers or considered his social status. Jesus always set his mind on pleasing the Father and counted it a privilege to do the will of God for His life.

Lydia, even as Christ did, found great satisfaction in serving God. Lydia's life still flourished after her conversion to Christianity. Her enthusiasm to serve was apparent in the way she quickly responded to the opportunity to open her home to the Apostle. God used her to help house the first Macedonian church in Philippi. We know from scripture that Christ longed to fulfill the will of God for his life. He allowed his desire to please his father in heaven to steer the course of his life. By doing so, Christ embraced the cross and died for our sins. He still rose on the third day and is now seated at the right hand of God. In Lydia's service, she exemplified a love to do the will of God and fulfill God's will for her life. In these ways, she emanated Christ through her service.

BIBIOGRAPGY

Charles, Rollin. "The History of The Lydians.". 1731

Emil G. Hirsch, George A. Barton."Cannan". Jewish Encyclopedia. 1906 ed. 2002-2011

Emil G. Hirsch, George A. Barton."SEMITES (originally Shemites)". Jewish Encyclopedia. 1906 ed.
2002-2011.

E. Hirsch, I. Price, W. Bacher, M. Seligsohn. "Shem". Jewish Encyclopedia. 1906 ed.
2002-2011.

Homer, A. T. Murray, and William F. Wyatt. Iliad. Cambridge, MA: Harvard UP, 1999.
Print.

Joseph Jacobs, M. Seligsohn."Ham." Jewish Encyclopedia. 1906 ed. 2002-2011.

Lockyer, Herbet. All The Women Of The Bible. Grand Rapid: Zondervan. 1967

Ockenge, Harold J. "Lydia — The Woman With the Open Heart

Orr, James, M.A., D.D. General Editor. "Entry for 'LUD; LUDIM'". "International Standard Bible Encyclopedia." 1915.

Orr, James, M.A., D.D. General Editor. "Entry for 'LYDIA (2)'". "International Standard Bible Encyclopedia."1915.

Pawsey, Tina. "Teaching for Women from the Bible - Women For The
Kingdom." Women from the Bible - Women For The Kingdom. N.p., n.d. Web. 22 July 2016.

Richard Gottheil, Louis H. Gray. "Hittites" Jewish Encyclopedia. 1906 ed. 2002-2011.

The Bible. Print. King James Vers.

Ham". The World Book Encyclopedia. Volume 9.1957. Print.

"Lydia"The World Book Encyclopedia Book. Volume 12.1957. Print.

"Macedonia" The World Book Encyclopedia. Volume 13.1957. Print.

"Philippi".The World Book Encyclopedia. Volume 15. 1957. Print

"Rome".The World Book Encyclopedia. Volume 16.1957. Print.

"Euodia." Wycliffe Bible Dictionary. Print

"Lydia." Wycliffe Bible Dictionary. Print.

"Occupation." Wycliffe Dictionary. Print.

"Women." Wycliffe Bible Dictionary. Print.

ABOUT THE AUTHOR

While attending college, A.D. Long began to feel a deeper call to ministry. She could relate to the lack of confidence she saw in her peers and understand the confusion media and opinions presented for those seeking their destiny. In her pursuit for ways to help, God began to deal with Long about using her vocation of fashion to reach out to others. Through Danny Girl Dresses, she creates opportunities for women and partners with other outreaches to assist beyond her locality. As an author and businesswomen, Long embraces every opportunity to motivate others to discover their identity through God's word.

"I found myself on a quest, like many, to figure out God's will for me. However, through much prayer, studying the word, and fellowship with other like-minded believers, I found my identity in Christ. I want to help other women do the same." -A.D. Long

To contact A.D. Long for other material, go to
www.adlongbooks.com

9 798736 997107